Living Purple Publishing
3651 S La Brea Avenue, Suite 610
Los Angeles, CA 90016

ISBN-13: 978-0-9968311-8-5
ISBN-10: 0-9968311-8-5
Library of Congress Control Number: 2019901051

For more information about selling or buying
properties in your local please visit
www.justfelloutofescrow.com

Published by Living Purple Publishing

JUST
FELL OUT
── OF ──
ESCROW

Top 5 reasons a property does not sell

Lisa Puerto

To the Property Owner/Seller – may you find confidence and comfort in learning what you can do to support the sale of your property in these next pages.

To the Buyer/Investor – See yourself as added value; rather than an advantage, to the transaction and use what you have learned here to take the necessary steps to safe guard your investment.

To the Agents and Industry Professionals – Thank you for reading and supporting this literary work as an important part of what you do in our industry. May you be inspired to continue to improve the real estate experience for us all.

- Super Agent®

*

By the way, if you prefer to skip the reading and want the short version...call my team.

We'll see you at the closing table.

800-676-1165 ext 807 – Sellers/Owners
800-676-1165 ext 808 –Buyers/Investors

DRE #01736957

CONTENTS

Preface

There is truly an art and excitement I get with negotiations, problem-solving and seeing clients win. My transactions have been litigious at times. I have even pondered maybe I should pursue becoming a real estate attorney. Ha! That was my childhood aspiration to be an attorney. After having been in the real industry for almost two decades (1st as a Notary Public – Loan Signing Agent) as a licensed California Real Estate Professional, I have always scrutinized contracts and questioned everything. It has been my innate passion to protect and serve those Buyers who were signing documents that they did not understand which led me in the direction I continue to pursue.

I gained more experience and consulted other professionals in their scenarios and real estate dealings. I observed how Sellers are often left uninformed of their own responsibilities to a transaction, which opened me up to seeing a serious need – Empower **all individuals** in the real estate transaction.

I have said on my platforms and will reiterate here; real estate is vicious – not for the faint at heart, it's cyclical, it can be emotional and draining without proper guidance, experience, and preparation.

This leads me to uncovering the ugly side of real estate in the following pages. The following reasons a property falls out of escrow, which essentially means a party to the transaction opted to cancel and back out of the deal. There is no particular order of importance, but can happen in any combination or might just show up as one underlying issue in a real estate transaction. As I share what those issues are, I offer ways to navigate through them successfully.

1.

Escrow

Before we jump right into what factors contribute to escrow falling apart, here's a word on Escrow. Depending where you are in the country, some real estate transactions are managed by a third-party agency such as escrow or a title company, or attorney also known as a settlement agent.

You actually owe it to yourself to meet these people in person if and when possible.

Fraud and embezzlement are real and prevalent because large increments of money are exchanged during a real estate transaction. While we want to believe that people are honest and trustworthy, there is extra care to consider when you are a Seller relying to get paid once the transaction has closed; a Buyer who is depositing your good faith deposit; a Lender who is wiring the financed part of the deal; and an Agent who is counting on getting paid from a successful closing.

Learn about what fees they charge, the services they offer and get an estimate of taxes due, closing escrow timelines and disbursement of funds. The team or staff at the escrow company or settlement agent you work with serves you and is there to assist you through the transaction. Request a Settlement estimate sheet so you can review the breakdown of costs associated with your transaction and always request why numbers are changed. Full disclosure is required and if at any time there are changes in the estimates, it is a potential for re-disclosures.

Escrow acts as a neutral third party with no interest and cannot/ nor should they provide advice on the negotiations advice to Seller or Buyer.

Escrow is the holder of two things: documents and money.

You have two choices of escrow to choose from. They can either be independently owned or non-independent (controlled) companies.

*

Independent Escrow

An independent escrow company has stringent requirements to be satisfied by the Department of Business Oversight. More importantly the amount of risk and liability for parties in a transaction is protected by requiring background check, fingerprinting, and audits of employees to this type of Escrow Company. Also, they are required to have someone onsite with at least 5 years of qualified escrow experience during business hours.

*

Non-Independent Escrow

Controlled companies are owned by a real estate brokerage, mortgage broker, and banks. They do not require background checks; or any work experience in escrow. While no background checks are required to determine whether someone has criminal activity or associated with misconduct, they are governed by the same laws as those overseeing real estate professionals, and title insurance companies. No bonds required to operate a controlled company.

I always negotiate to work with an Independent Escrow company because I have seen how it can be difficult to manage a transaction and protect my client while working with a controlled escrow company that may be owned or an affiliate to the real estate brokerage, mortgage broker, and banks. Again, we want to believe that everyone will act ethically however, the fact that we have seen markets crash and continue to see the unethical practices of some brokerages, agents, and banks we should always proceed with caution.

As a real estate professional, it is part of the deal we all look forward to whether it's a sounding board or email confirmation reading:

JUST OPENED ESCROW

JUST FUNDED

JUST RECORDED

...as opposed to hearing it the other way

JUST FELL OUT OF ESCROW

CANCELED ESCROW

But, if it is the latter, this now creates an opportunity to put the deal back together for a win-win-win. Through the course of my deals I have chosen the higher road at times because if the goal is to serve the client, albeit seeing homeownership a reality for first gen'ers or a Seller who really needs to sell their home and move on with the next chapter in their lives, it is important to me to see how best we can get both sides of the transaction to the closing table. On some deals, it has cost me money, meaning a portion of my own commission to chip in. I have assisted clients all the way through not just in service, but also putting my money where my mouth is – getting it done!

Not all deals require this and there are creative ways to manage it. I have just been one to meet the needs of people and in turn have been entrusted by my clients for life. And for me, this is how I turn a one-time transaction to a life-time of referral business.

2.

Repair nEGOtiations

Repairs can be a tricky part of the real estate transaction to navigate. I will section this off into three different parts because it may get confusing as I discuss what repairs are required and which ones are not: City Pre-sale Inspections, Home Inspections, and Lender Required Repairs.

Repairs also can set the tone for the real estate transaction once an offer is accepted and terms and conditions are agreed upon. How? If Seller states that they are selling the property AS-IS and will not agree to the pre-sale inspection or any lender required repairs, can damper the homeownership aspirations for a first-time buyer. I also strongly recommend Buyer Beware if you are not experienced in dealing with City Pre-sale Inspections and/or need to complete Lender Required Repairs.

*

City Pre-sale Inspections

Not all Pre-sale Inspections Are Created Equal.

Pre-sale Inspections are designed to protect Buyers of residential property against any undisclosed building code violations on the property. Also, depending on the city, it can delay closing escrow if not ordered and completed in a timely manner. So imagine, having satisfied all terms of the sale and the lender is ready to fund the loan, ah-but wait, you can't! Why? Escrow is not allowed to close the file without satisfying the pre-sale inspection requirements. Here is how you get the deal closed with full disclosure to all parties.

Check the city in which the property is located to learn what the local ordinances are regarding pre-sale city inspection requirements. The city building and safety department often has a requirement of minimum state law compliances for property condition that have to deal with health and safety. For example, smoke detectors, carbon monoxide detectors, water heaters being properly strapped and earth quake shut-off valve need to be installed.

As a real estate professional, I recommend contracting a retrofitting company that can satisfy the city requirements and more importantly is qualified to sign off on the Compliance Certificate. The retrofitters that I have worked with are nice enough to suggest to my clients what would be more cost effective.

On the other hand, other city pre-sale inspections will issue a Corrections Notice. The Pre-sale Corrections List may require that repairs/replacements, and permits be verified or pulled for any modifications, installations, renovations completed to the exterior, electrical, water heater, plumbing, mechanical, garage, and any miscellaneous items of a property. There are two options to navigating this scenario:

(1) Full Compliance: The Seller or Buyer if agreed to in the purchase contract or in any addendums to the purchase

contract will comply with all items called out by the City Inspector, **or**

(2)   AS-IS: This often is expensive if the Correction List involves permits or demolition of any additions, which will derail the transaction and will require the Seller and Buyer to seriously consider the cost and liability incurred if waiving compliance. It does not mean that the list of repairs is ignored, but rather states that either the Seller or Buyer will be responsible for compliance after close of escrow in order to satisfy a release. Be advised, the City's Building and Safety will require that any violations are addressed within 30 days after closing escrow, and if not satisfied in a timely manner, a lien will be placed against the property. This however, does not prohibit an

extension of time needed to complete the work.

If you are not familiar with pre-sale inspections, you just got a dose of it and from experience; it can be overwhelming if not scheduled in a timely manner. Escrow is riding on timelines and contingencies and depending on how the Seller and Buyer compromise or not...can result in a property falling out of escrow.

*

Professional Home Inspections

It is highly recommended that a Buyer get a professional inspection on a prospective property. This is done within their inspection contingency timeframe of the purchase contract, and is essentially their 'walk-out' if the property does not meet their standards or feel they might be in way over their head. With that being said, the Buyer's Request for Repairs are for their due diligence and the Seller is NOT required to cure or correct any items listed on the home inspection report. In the industry, it is better known as a Buyer's Wish List. Try explaining that to a first-time buyer. Not easy, but necessary. Any repairs or replacements found on professional inspection reports can be dealt with in the following ways:

(1) Seller agrees to fix all or some items

(2) Seller does not agree to fix any items and will offer a repair credit, or better written as '**credit for non-recurring closing costs**.'[1]

---

[1] Check with the Buyer/Borrower's Lender to determine the amount of credit issued does not exceed what is allowable for the loan and the verbiage has to be stated in such a way

(3) Seller can reject all items and offer a price reduction per Buyer request

(4) Seller can reject all items and not issue any credits or price reduction

At any time during this stage of negotiation, YOU are <u>still negotiating</u>. It does not end once the initial offer is accepted. Remember when I mentioned the contract terms and conditions sets the tone of the transaction — this is exactly where ego rears its head. And from experience, it can be from any side of the transaction, seller, buyer, or agents, who are negotiating on matters from cosmetic repairs, replacing fixtures, major repairs, or any number of things that may have been disclosed on the home inspection report.

Home inspections are disclaimed as a general inspection and if specialty inspections are recommended that too should be completed at the expense of the Buyer. If specialty inspections are done, and any issues are found, the Buyer's list of repairs just got expensive. If neither side can come to an agreement and compromise on terms of dealing with repairs, then Buyer or Seller can cancel the deal, and back on market (BOM) the property goes, with a little tag line that says: JUST FELL OUT OF ESCROW!!!! [Sometimes with that many exclamation points] We will discuss the significance of that in the last chapter.

*

Lender Required Repairs

If you thought the home inspection was bumpy, saddle up: Lenders require properties meet minimum conditions as set forth by the HUD guidelines. It is important that a property is insurable when using the FHA insured or VA guaranty loans.

(1) FHA Appraisals: This may sound very confusing if you are new to appraisal inspections because you would typically associate 'appraisal' with valuations. True. And in the case of **FHA insured loans**[2] it also refers to repairs needed. For example, peeling paint needs to be cured, or a roof needing to have a remaining life of minimum 2 years, water heater needs to be strapped, etc.

---

[2] FHA Insured Loans also known as the 'First-time buyer' program commonly used by first-time buyer(s) who have a minimum of 3.5% down payment or are highly encumbered meaning carry high debt-to-income ratios. HUD guidelines states that a First-time buyer is a borrower who has not held a mortgage or written off the mortgage interest deduction on their taxes within the last 3 years

(2) VA Appraisals: While the VA loan program is a great purchase program for military veterans, it also has stringent requirements regarding condition of a property before funding the loan. For example, be prepared to provide a termite clearance certificate. Termites are not your friend as a property owner because they literally are eating away your asset. Once the termite inspection has been completed and copy of the report is issued into escrow it becomes part of the transaction and requires full disclosure to all parties with vested interest. Section I of the Termite report has to be resolved prior to close of escrow. Note, in California purchases termite clearances are not required unless written into the purchase contract.

Depending on what the Appraisal Reports call out during the inspection, will determine how once again, you negotiate repairs.

The difference with this list of repairs is without clearing those Lender Required Repairs the Buyer/Borrower will be unable to get the loan. In the event that your negotiation is at a stalemate consider dealing with repairs with either a Repair Escrow, or FHA 203k. The repair escrow cannot exceed repair estimates of $5,000 and requires a 1.5 contingency. Check lender guidelines regarding this contingency. If the Seller, Buyer, or Agents are unable to agree on how to resolve those issues...you guessed it, the Seller or Buyer can cancel the contract and there goes another property that: JUST FELL OUT OF ESCROW.

Each repair negotiation scenario is unique to each transaction and depends on the goal of each party in moving forward with successfully working through it. Often times, a **First-time Home Seller**[3] who has never experienced escrow from that side of a transaction will feel completely overwhelmed and will opt to cancel without pursuing further negotiations.

The same applies to a First-time Buyer, who has felt like the repairs may not justify the agreed upon price and may opt to cancel the contract. Without knowing the specifics of each transaction, I will limit offering suggestions here on how to work through it. Just know each party, including Agents, can contribute to solutions that result in a win-win-win.

---

[3] Stoked to share my next book will focus on being a specific resource to property owners and heirs 'First-time Home Sellers: From Keys to Proceeds' tenantive release date Aug.2019

3.

Appraisals

Pricing a property in any market requires strategy and due diligence. It is important to be mindful of the types of financing used to purchase a property. You learned in Chapter 1 how Lender Required Repairs can affect the transaction if the property condition is not properly taken into consideration prior to acceptance.

Appraisals are used for valuations and when a property is being financed the property must appraise at contract price or more.

No loan, no home.

What if the property does not appraise? And it happens, and more often

right when the market begins to shift downward . . .

Yikes, if you get caught right in the middle of a market attempting to price correct. It may be necessary to request another appraisal as a second opinion, or even a third to factor in variables that maybe were not considered in the original appraisal.

In the event that the appraisal comes back below the contract price – the Seller and Buyer have the following options to consider:

> (1) Seller can request that the Buyer make up the price difference between the contract price and the appraised value. For this reason, submitting over asking price in a multiple offer scenario can be

risky because if the Seller requests that the Buyer make-up the difference and has indicated a **clause**[4] in the Seller Counter Offer (SCO) or any Addendums to the Purchase Contract, the Buyer will be locked in or risks losing their deposit if they cannot perform.

(2) Buyer can request that the Seller reduce the price to the appraised value. This is where it can get sticky because a Seller may not want to reduce the price with hopes that they can consider a back-up offer, or another offer with similar price and terms. This won't pan out the way they imagine specifically because depending on the market and property location, it is common to see

---

[4] No Appraisal Contingency is an example of a clause that could potentially lock in a Buyer into purchasing the property regardless of the appraised value – There is a way around this, but you will have to contact me directly to learn my strategy or assist with negotiations

certain types of financing used to purchase property.

For example, if the Buyer in escrow is using an FHA insured loan, and the FHA appraisal determined the value to be less than the contract price, that valuation is assigned an FHA Case Number that remains with that property for 6 months. Um, so unless you are in an area where the Buyer clientele is using another type of financing, there is no way around this valuation. Try waiting for 6 months in hopes that the price goes up. Good luck.

In short, review other areas of the deal that may have over extended the Seller, for example if they may have issued closing costs credits and it would be better suited for a price reduction. If Seller, Buyer, nor Agent can come to terms on the valuation – yep, contract canceled: JUST FELL OUT OF ESCROW!

4.

Tenant Relocations and Evictions

At the time of writing this book there was a Bill in California on the ballot that would subject Single Family Residences (SFR) to rent control. Yes, depending on what side of the coin you are on it could be detrimental or victorious. The result; It did not pass and therefore still remains a very important part of a real estate transaction to negotiate when a property has occupants. I will section this off discussing Single Family Residences and **Multi-family Residences**[5]

*

Single Family Residence (SFR)

This is the good, bad, and ugly of real estate transactions. Not all tenants are created equal and it is with full disclaimer that as a real estate professional I recommend you ask pertinent questions about the status of tenant relocation when considering a property with tenants. If the property purchased is for Owner-Occupied, meaning the Buyer intends to live in it as their primary residence,

---

[5] Residential real estate is considered 1-4 units. For this example, I will only limit the discussion to residential and not go into negotiations of commercial real estate and tenant scenarios because the Buyer/Investor profile and financing options are drastically different

establish tenant timelines immediately. It is customary and within legal grounds to give a tenant a 60 day notice to relocate. It is not required to offer relocation money to a tenant, but if necessary proceed with caution on the terms.

In a perfect world, a tenant is cooperative and will allow a prospective Buyer to complete their due diligence inspections, they will maintain the property in move-in condition for the new owner and all is well. *Peaches and cream, ha-ha.*

And then in the real world (more times than I would like to see this happen) tenants will fight you to the end with hopes of sabotaging a real estate transaction so that they do not move or the property does not sell. A word about what motivates a tenant to do such thing: their housing.is.at.stake. Period. Often times they have been residing in the home for years, a comfortable space they may have grown into and have been paying below or current market rents.

When a tenant does an aggressive takeover of a property, the legal and ethical way of dealing with it is to evict the tenant. No, the Seller cannot kick them out, change the locks, and turn off the utilities. DO NOT under any circumstance as a Seller or Agent get involved in menacing activities to force a tenant out.

Who handles the eviction? If the Seller agreed to a clause or condition of the purchase contract to **deliver vacant**[6], then they have signed for the responsibility and liability associated with evicting their tenants.

---

[6] If agreeing to deliver property vacant at close of escrow, be sure to research eviction attorneys with a positive track record of successfully evicting tenants, and avoid using the *cheap evictions* services because it may end up being more costly in the long-run

If this process becomes long and drawn out, a Buyer may opt to not wait and cancel the contract, and there is nothing a Seller can do and there goes another one: JUST FELL OUT OF ESCROW

*

Multi-Family Residence

In the event that the property has more than one unit, the Buyer will only require at least one of the units be delivered vacant. Because the property is a multi-family residence, it can be subject to rent control, thereby requiring the tenant(s) be paid to relocate. This can be expensive, upward to $25,000 depending on how long the tenant has occupied the unit and whether they are seniors, disabled, and/or have minor children.

The Buyer can wait up to 90 days post-closing escrow before occupying the property as required by most loans. This could give a Buyer time to relocate the tenant if they opt to take on the relocation.

Without properly factoring in this cost, a real estate transaction can easily be derailed and a Buyer may opt out of wanting to take on the costs to pay relocation if a Seller is unwilling to do so. The end result:

JUST FELL OUT OF ESCROW

> This section factors in owner-occupied purchases because the financing is qualified differently than a non-owner occupied purchase. Tenant retention and evaluating upside potential of an investment would have to be factored in with careful analysis.

5.

Borrower's Credit or Income Profile

This is the easiest way to get an escrow to fall out just as quickly as it opened. There is a difference between a Pre-qualification, Pre-approval, and TBD Approval.

When an offer is accepted, a Buyer will then receive a Loan Estimate based on the contract price. Two things happen:

    (1) Sticker shock: A Buyer/Borrower will not expect to see the additional fees associated with closing their purchase and the estimated mortgage payment will shock/scare them into not wanting to move forward. It happens. It's a real

commitment. Not for the faint of heart, remember? And they cancel escrow. This is not only about proper preparation from both Lender and Agent to their Buyer client, but also requires an open discussion about how the Agent is negotiating price, terms, and concessions (i.e. Buyer's closing costs credits)

(2) Buyer's remorse: A Buyer/Borrower feels like the large investment they are about to commit to is a mistake or completely unnerving. Any kind of change for humans is stressful. And if they are unwilling to work pass this feeling, they will cancel the contract.

I opened this chapter with the types of qualifications and approvals a Borrower can attain during the home buying process because they are not created equal.

The least intrusive into a Buyer's finances and ability to purchase is a Pre-qualification letter. The credit score is not run and no loan application is completed.

Pre-approval requires credit report, income and asset verification to determine purchasing power.

TBD Approval requires full documentation, is submitted to the loan underwriter for a conditional loan approval pending the purchase contract, preliminary title, and appraisal.

If the Buyer is not properly vetted prior to executing a purchase contract, the surprise during escrow could be that the Borrower is unable to qualify for the contract price. And you will see that infamous line: JUST

FELL OUT OF ESCROW, with an added note of 'no fault of seller.'

How to navigate this scenario? Easy, require that a Buyer submit a DU approval or a pre-approval from a Direct Lender. And as a Buyer, know the difference and you are not required to complete cross-qualifications[7].

A Buyer's credit can send a deal crashing because as many times as real estate professionals we advise our clients not to open any new credit accounts or incur any additional debt while they are in escrow, they might have a bill that somehow appears out of nowhere. Go figure?

---

[7] Cross-qualifications are when an Agent/Seller requests that a Buyer go through the loan qualification process with a 'Preferred Lender' - Be advised there is a fine line with doing so because it may border steering a Buyer which is against the law

Depending on the loan type, the Lender will run the credit before loan documents are drawn for the Buyer to sign and if there is a decrease in the FICO score – game over.

At that point there is not much that can be done to reconcile the new scoring without having to wait an additional 30 days. And realistically, if escrow is set to close 72 hours, who wants to wait another 30 days because the Buyer's credit profile changed. If there are other variables in a transaction such as a close concurrent, or a Seller needing to close within a certain time frame, could create a liability, and risk a Buyer's deposit because they are unable to perform within the contracted time. As part of a complete offer package, Agents often request a copy of the pre-approval with credit score and proof of funds to deter a contract from falling out of escrow.

6.

Net Proceeds

You may have skipped right to this section, it's okay. I get it. Ultimately, you can resolve repair negotiations, get passed egos, buyers' remorse, appraisals, tenants relocations or evictions, do a rapid rescore on a credit profile, maybe even add a non-occupant borrower to assist with qualifying for the property if the income profile needs to be adjusted for … and still run into an issue with not having enough money in the deal to close escrow. A Seller may have an existing mortgage, or an order for child support/alimony, IRS/State Tax Lien, or undisclosed personal loans that will throw a wrench in the numbers. What now? Depending on the agency or the position of the lien holder, they have to get their money right off the top. Meaning, they must be paid from the Seller's Net Proceeds and if there is not enough money in the transaction once commissions and escrow fees, and seller concessions are factored in – you have no deal. And just like that, another one bites the dust: JUST FELL OUT OF ESCROW

These are the 11th hour scenarios that can be avoided if you 'front-load' a transaction, find out all debts upfront and ask the questions of the Seller if you can to disclose any and all debts. Same goes for the Buyer. If the Buyer has any debts or liens that come up during a title search, it must be satisfied before a lender will fund the loan.

I have had my own transactions reveal an undisclosed loan that the Seller did not disclose. What happens next? You get it done. The responsibility is that of the representing Agent to collect the necessary information for Escrow, often times on the Statement of Information.

It will be at the discretion of the title and escrow company to either hold a portion of the Seller's proceeds to satisfy any liens and still close escrow. Again, that is at their discretion and based often on relationships. It is important to work with reputable closing companies to assist with successfully closing escrow.

7.

Create a Winning Opportunity

Getting through escrow is the goal. Of course
it is. No one purposely wants to fall out of
escrow. As a real estate professional it's the
last thing I want our clients to experience.
However, there are so many moving parts in
a transaction that cannot be controlled that
will end up thwarting the deal. How we
respond to the falling apart can make you or
break you. I have been one to take on
challenges in my personal life and face it.
Same applies to my professional life.

My clients' are relying on my team to get them through their purchases and we continue to do so successfully.

If you are a property owner, thinking about Selling I trust that the information I have shared will help you navigate some pitfalls to avoid. You are responsible for what you can control in the transaction. I offer a Free consultation for your property to see what options are available to meet the needs of the sale.

*

SELLERS/OWNERS

If you are a Seller who has fallen out of escrow; I extend an opportunity to reach out to our team to connect with eligible Buyers who can purchase your property Cash and as-is condition. The clients we work with use financing that is underwritten by reputable direct lenders that have reviewed a Buyer's financials and guarantee the loan in the form of a non-contingent loan[8]. Not all lenders can perform on this type of loan and not all agents can negotiate an offer with this contract condition. The advantages of working with these types of Buyers are your contracts are written with shorter timelines for inspections and removal of contingencies without risking another escrow to a long drawn out process. Pay attention to the good faith deposit a Buyer offers because it reveals a *good faith* of how much 'skin in the game' they are willing to offer. Delivery of the deposit is what makes a fully executed contract; without the deposit

---

[8] Non-contingency loans: Do not attempt to write an offer without the professional experience of a real estate professional and a Direct Lender that has a proven track record to perform on this contract condition

in escrow, you have no deal even if you have a signed agreement. Our focus is to create a winning scenario because we are sensitive to timelines and your needs of having gone through the ups and downs of escrow.

*

BUYERS/INVESTORS

For prospective Buyers and or Investors looking for opportunity to *save the deal* – you are needed. As you have learned through the preceding chapters, a real estate deal now has preliminary title reports, home inspection reports, city reports, and at times appraisals that have already been completed while in escrow. That's a cost savings to you because you can request to review those reports as part of your due diligence inspections. What that means to you? Cost-savings and unlike the previous Buyer, you now know what you are getting yourself into without having to spend on those inspections and reports. If you are getting your loan financed, your respective Lender will require their appraisal unless it's an FHA appraisal. See Chapter 3 Appraisals for my notes on that.

You are now equipped with negotiating power and a Seller is now more apt to consider your offer because on average they have been on the market for 21 days during the escrow period. You have enough information to feel confident to save the deal and create a winning opportunity for your first-time purchase or repeat deal.

*

Agents/Industry Professionals

Your fiduciary responsibility is to your client(s). Find ways to support them through their real estate sale/purchase. The difference between most clients and us is we do this for a living, and they will on average do this once or twice in their liftetime. They are relying on us to make the escrow experience as professional and ethical as possible for all parties. I extend myself as a resource for consult to negotiate your deal through to closing.

We'll see you at the closing table.

~ Super Agent®

Lisa Puerto, Super Agent®

California Licensed Real Estate Professional, also known as Super Agent®, International Speaker, Public Educator AND more importantly Founder of our nation's first real estate focused nonprofit for youth and young adults.

Real Estate 100 Youth Foundation Inc.

The mission of 'RE100' seeks to empower youth ages 11-17 with real estate terms, concepts, and careers as an alternate pathway to success! Learn more about how you can support by visiting www.realestate100youth.org

Creator and Host of Ready, Set, REAL ESTATE® - The show is a digital footprint of the diverse people of color in all aspects of the real estate industry. Special Millennial Guests featured.

Lisa is widely known for her trailblazing

book, **Real Estate 100: The Teen Home Buying Experience** (2015) which is the first genre of real estate literacy for youth.

Host of Ready, Set, REAL ESTATE!®
Founder of Real Estate 100 Youth Foundation Inc.
Creator and Author of the *Real Estate 100* book series, Property Owner Edu, 2019 Millenials Real Estate Summit, and co-creator of the Spirit of Business miniCourse™

2018 Award Winning Author
2018 Leading Lady Prodigy Award Recipient
National Women in Real Estate Business

Let's get social. @lasuperagent
Facebook Instagram YouTube Twitter LinkedIN

Subscribe to the show on radio podcast
everywhere and <u>YouTube.com/lasuperagent</u>:
Ready, Set, REAL ESTATE!®
<u>Spotify</u> <u>Google Play Music</u> iTunes <u>Stitcher Radio</u>

DRE #01736957

Look for these titles by the author

Real Estate 100: The Teen Home Buying Experience (2015)

Real Estate 100: The Teen and Millennial Investment Blueprint (2017)

Ready, Set, Real Estate: How to when the market shifts (2018)

First-time Home Sellers: From Keys to Proceeds (2019)

Bookings

Contact info@realestate100.net for packages, sponsorship opportunities, and special pricing on books.

Press Kit with speaking schedules included for reference

www.ingramcontent.com/pod-product-compliance
Lightning Source LLC
Chambersburg PA
CBHW020845210326
41598CB00019B/1985